ALL THINGS CONSIDERED

*Thoughtful interior design that mixes
pattern, colour and style*

EMILIO PIMENTEL-REID

Photography by Edvinas Bruzas

Quadrille

CONTENTS

4 / Introduction

8 / Willow Kemp / Chelsea, London

22 / Philip Hooper / Clapham, London

40 / J.J. Martin / Milan, Italy

58 / Gert Voorjans / Antwerp, Belgium,

74 / Rodman Primack & Rudy Weissenberg / Lomas de Chapultepec, Mexico City

90 / Timothy Corrigan / 16ième, Paris

110 / Michal Silver / Chelsea, London

124 / Patrick Williams & Neriman Kamcili / Bath, Somerset

142 / Holly Howe / Dartmouth Park, London

158 / Anthony Collett / Shepherd's Bush, London

176 / Sasha Bikoff / West Village, New York City

188 / Sophie Dries / 4ième, Paris

204 / Alexandra Tolstoy / Cotswolds, Oxfordshire

222 / Natalia Miyar / Coral Gables, Florida

240 / Jennifer Shorto / Kensington, London

252 / Francis Sultana / Mayfair, London

270 / Credits

270 / Acknowledgements

INTRODUCTION

As a UK-based design author and creative strategist, I come into contact with top designers across the world. The idea for this book came from my regular conversations with them, and from my desire to reveal how these international creatives are fashioning highly personal interiors for themselves, as well as to explore the relationship we all have with our homes. This book highlights distinctive spaces: some historically influenced and others at the cutting edge of contemporary design, some serene and several provocative, but all uplifting and created with great thought, confidence and flair. In the mix of moods, colours, patterns, objects and textures that can be seen in the inspiring interiors across these pages, all things have been very thoughtfully considered – leaving room for style, surprise, joy and personality.

To widen the scope of the visual conversation in *All Things Considered* and to share with you a variety of homes, I have focused on a mix of designers from the UK and influential design capitals across the rest of Europe and in North America, all at the top of their game. Each designer shines for their original style of decoration and the bold mix of elements they incorporate into their interiors. *All Things Considered* is not about one point of view or look, but rather about encountering accomplished spaces built on integrity, gut feeling, deep knowledge and great personality. You will find that the book highlights creatives at different stages in their professional careers, from those who are just being discovered, through those who are established, to a few legendary names who are still leaders in the industry. They all have inspiring viewpoints to share.

As someone passionate about homes, still filled with curiosity after 25 years exploring and promoting design, I have found that often the most alluring and successful interiors are those that designers conceive for themselves. Perhaps this is because they experiment at home before deploying their ideas on clients, or because they take risks that they might not in professional projects. At home, also, they often tackle challenges that are not faced by their clients: budget or size of space, maybe, or the even tougher challenge of committing to design choices for oneself. Each designer has approached their interior differently – just as you should.

The 16 homes featured in this book constitute a celebration of individuality, an uplifting collection of interiors that mix varied elements with gusto to create joyful spaces. We have highlighted nine of the qualities that make each interior unique in the *All Things Considered* page. In real life we are all very different – at different stages of our lives, with different passions and taste – and designers are just like us, except with great expertise. They are all highly knowledgeable about the zeitgeist at any given moment, yet refreshingly admit to not caring about trends. This liberating outlook leads to interiors that have great longevity, because they are made just for their owners. These artists, gallerists, designers and other creatives with varied backgrounds value a strong sense of personality above all else.

I hope you will be inspired by these great mixologists. Not with drinks, of course, but blending personality and style to encourage you to celebrate your individuality and create interiors that are very *You* – all things considered.

EMILIO PIMENTEL-REID
Bath, England

WILLOW KEMP / *Chelsea, London*

'I greet most people slightly out of breath after they have climbed the stairs to the top of the building,' says interior architect Willow Kemp of her joyful flat in the upper reaches of a converted building dating from 1884, in the Park Carlyle Conservation Area of London's Chelsea. 'But I always love the look of surprise on their faces when they arrive!'

Visitors also comment on how spacious it feels. Willow – an art ambassador for her family's Firmdale Hotels and design director at Kit Kemp Design Studio – has managed to claim an extra 0.6 m (2 ft) in ceiling height by opening up the loft space. Decorated with the flair of an artist and the know-how of a top designer at the cult hotel brand, the flat combines her passion for collecting contemporary art (some of it fresh from graduate shows) and fascinating objects with a technical understanding of architecture. Injected with Willow's love of colour and pattern, the flat deploys all the practicality, space-saving tricks and sense of occasion of a well-conceived hotel suite, balancing the owner's precision and spirited personality. This means that in a smallish space there's room for a dining table for six; the bed is jump-up princess height; and the compact kitchen/hallway is functional and stylish enough to be in full view.

Willow's home is fresh and liveable, with artworks that tell a story of her trips, interests and life. A connective creative thread runs through all the spaces. The rug in the living room, for example, was the inspiration for 'One Way', a fabric design that she worked on for Kit Kemp's collection with the textile and wallpaper designer Christopher Farr, and which is on the walls in the entrance and up the staircase. The attention to subtle detail – pops of coloured piping, contrasting leather and a handle at the top of dining chairs, studding on furniture where two materials meet – brings added interest.

The building was originally artists' studios occupied by landscape painters, and has a distinctive Arts and Crafts appearance, being constructed from red brick with white stucco decoration to the entrance portico. 'My flat on the top floor has a beautiful, large, full-width bay window to the east and vertical sash windows to the north and south, making it especially light and airy,' explains Willow. 'I love how you feel in touch with Chelsea's past, when there was a concentration of artists' studios.' In the bedroom, she often paints at a 19th-century rosewood heirloom desk with delightful cardboard lamps by Biarritz artist Mimi Chanard and a view of Chelsea beyond.

The flat is a place for Willow to display her various collections so that the pieces have a dialogue with one another, giving the space character, energy and soul. 'When I come home from a long day at work,' she says, 'I love to open the door to my happy home. I often sit at the window seats I made by extending the windowsills and adding a tailored cushion. I'm up in the eaves, so the curtains swing back and are lined with a ticking fabric. I can peer over at the south-facing leafy gardens or into my open-plan living room and kitchen filled with light from the original studio window.'

'Walking around Chelsea, I often spot blue plaques testifying to the numerous historical figures that have lived in the area, and I'm reminded of their accomplishments and imagine them once living in my neighbourhood.'

'I'm interested in scale and balance, and try to accentuate the best features of a space. I play with texture, pattern and material in a way that makes you want to do a double take. You can't possibly figure out a room in one visit.'

JUXTAPOSITION / *It's all about scale and balance, and just trying out different compositions.*

BALANCE / *I'm always playing around with my collections of objects,*
whether they be ceramics, a handwoven basket or a pair of timber running horses found on my
travels. Each piece evokes its own memory, has its own story to tell and its own particular place,
otherwise it would look disjointed and not feel right to me.

SURPRISE / *Pairing old and new can give an object a new lease of life.*
I have mixed traditional hand-embroidered fabrics with bold, graphic ones. I have a traditional
oil painting next to a 3D timber collage of a seagull's head. I have cut out a bookshelf to make
way for a large plaster cast of a lion's head.

COLOUR / *Colour makes me happy. I chose to line the walls with a neutral fabric,*
giving it a tailored feel, and let the happy blues and touches of red in the upholstered
furniture fabrics and the artworks sing. In my bedroom, I have chosen one of my favourite
fabrics, 'Kos' hand-embroidered linen by Vaughan, featuring fir cone-like details stitched
in golden, bronze and earthy tones of thread.

PATTERN / *I have played with scale, but the spaces still feel calm. Where I have used*
a large-scale [pattern] repeat, it is balanced with smaller-scale ones, and plains.

TEXTURE / *Texture is so important. I have used linens, embroidery, leather and weaves.*
Different materials provide different textures: beautiful light-coloured timber floors, and antique
mirror in the kitchen splashback and behind the bookshelves.

MOOD / *Bright and light in look and feeling.*

LIMITATIONS & POSSIBILITIES / *I made my flat open-plan. I was careful to make sure the*
curtains were designed and hung so that they maximise the amount of light inside. Antique mirror
in recesses and uplit behind the bookshelves reflects light and makes the space feel larger.

ALL THINGS CONSIDERED / *My home reflects me and where I am in my life at the moment.*
I'm a happy, creative and curious person.

PHILIP HOOPER / *Clapham, London*

Philip Hooper, joint managing director of Britain's longest-established interior-decorating firm, Sibyl Colefax & John Fowler, lives on the border between Clapham and Brixton Hill in south London. The area surrounding his apartment in a converted Victorian school is a cheek-by-jowl mix of expensive period homes and social housing. Philip's neighbourhood reflects this energy, with the small, specialist food vendors of Brixton an easy walk away and the Michelin-starred restaurants of Clapham Common in the other direction. It all seems very London still, and not overly gentrified.

Having trained as an architect before becoming an interior decorator, Philip has a background that enables him to think about everything from the foundations upwards, and his skill as a draughtsman gives him the ability to clearly convey ideas visually. A fascinating man at the top of the international design scene, he comes across as gentle and welcoming, fiercely intelligent and generous with his deep knowledge of design.

In this brick conversion, the classrooms are now lofty apartments, with high ceilings and huge windows that give a faintly industrial feel. The developers sold the units as empty space – basically one big classroom – and in his, Philip has put everything where he wanted it. 'With my architectural upbringing, the opportunity to create a space from scratch and specifically for my needs was ideal,' he explains. 'I designed the apartment solely for me as a London base, my pied-à-terre. My apartment doesn't cater to others' idiosyncrasies; I can have my books and my desk, and have everything open.'

Philip's home is well edited, bringing together pieces from different cultures and periods. 'There is a selection of random objects that is given coherence as they are filtered through me,' he says. 'The fact that it's one's own interests, love and vision gives them continuity, and the fact that they all have a story to tell, and that story is part of my world.' He liked the idea of living in a loft – or as close as you can get to one in London. Here is one of the UK's top design talents, used to working on grand projects across the globe, packing his ingenuity into a relatively small space that slowly unfolds to the eye.

Beyond being his pied-à-terre, the apartment is a space to show paintings. It is really one big open-plan studio, so no single corner outshines another. 'I wanted to create a modern loft space that had strong architectural form,' he explains, 'full of surprises and a foil for my mid-century art and furniture. I wanted to be modern but not predictable, by using colour and pattern. Modernism isn't just about white spaces. Colour was a background for pictures and objects, and I introduced texture. At the time that I first did this apartment, people weren't using colour in that way in this sort of interior. I wanted to take the shape and idea of that modern look, which was simple, and use colour as embellishment. I added the colour and softness as someone who wanted to marry interior decoration with interior architecture.'

Because no one else is involved and no other person had to give an opinion, this is completely Philip's own space. Working for yourself is a unique opportunity, he says: 'It's not like working for anyone else. People who visit are fascinated by the fact that every single thing has a story, from the ceramics to the art and furniture. These are stories of my shopping over the years, my inquisitiveness and my patronising of contemporary makers.'

'We are all governed by proportion and geometry, these are key. You become a mannerist with an ability to understand the rules and, over time, sufficiently dextrous to bend them. If you are fluent in history and design, architecture gets turned around to create something different and more cerebral, and through that knowledge you also have the confidence to reinvent.'

'Do not pander to fashion. It's irrelevant. Set a brief and stick to it. Modern interior design is not about white walls and minimalism, it's about sculpting your space.'

JUXTAPOSITION / *I have a desire to be surrounded by things that evoke memories and stories. The thread of my love for a place or an object is what unifies them.*

BALANCE / *Every few years I add and subtract furniture and objects, and rehang pictures. The apartment is always too full, but I have plenty of storage, so things can be exiled from view.*

SURPRISE / *The key is to keep the interior as a cabinet of curiosities with no real theme. Part of the visual trickery is that you come in through a relatively small entrance hall that reveals a big open space. There are areas that are partitioned off and discovered as you walk through the apartment.*

COLOUR / *This hasn't changed much over the years. The mix of white and darker, earthy tones was always a foil for my pictures, some of which suit different backgrounds. Colours recur in different areas, so your eye can pick up on the continuity and the common themes.*

PATTERN / *I aimed to restrict the pattern to one area that was not always visible; finding it was part of the puzzle. I saw an image of the wallpaper in a magazine, and it stuck with me, so I wanted to find a vehicle for it. I wanted to use the yellow and white and the black. My use of that particular paper was a catalyst for the way I started to put other things together.*

TEXTURE / *I imagined the volumes and walls as a kind of puzzle box, or a Russian doll. Architecturally my design is about planes and constructivist shapes, all of which have a different colour or finish. There isn't really a lot of texture. I continue to add to and play with the space. The leather panelling behind the bed was salvaged from a shop on Bond Street; it came later, to give a different feel to the view from one side of the hallway to the other.*

MOOD / *The apartment is bohemian modernist, achieved through daring and experimentation. The layout is open-plan – even the bathroom – which is a very un-English way of thinking. That was me coming outside the normal restraints that you set yourself as a designer. I kept the materials simple; for example, the wood is the same as the floor, and the green slate colour in keeping with the overall palette. In the bathroom, the wood is a strong tropical red, which comes from the Art Deco side of things, like the designs of Émile-Jacques Ruhlmann.*

LIMITATIONS & POSSIBILITIES / *I ignored the limitations.*

ALL THINGS CONSIDERED / *I enjoy that my apartment is all about me.*

The city of Milan has a multitude of different architectural styles: so-so post-war buildings, gems from the 1960s, 1920s fascist architecture, 18th- and 19th-century treasures, as well as those in the Liberty style, Italy's version of Art Nouveau. 'I've always been attracted to the older parts of Milan,' says American-born J.J. Martin, founder and creative director of La DoubleJ, the fashion and homeware label known for its unapologetic maximalism plied with joy. 'The street I live on is perhaps my favourite in the city,' she says. 'It's planted along its whole length with big, beautiful trees, a rarity in Milan, and is conveniently close to the park that I love, so I can walk my pug dog, Pepper, every morning. I really lucked into the place – I'd been searching for the perfect apartment forever and finally just walked down to this area that I knew I loved and started talking to all the doormen, asking if any apartments were available. Milan can be very bureaucratic, and some things can be slow. I took matters into my own hands and suddenly it all felt right. By chance this one was available. Homes to me are so important. I'm sensitive to the environment, as a Taurus – we are very tied to the home.'

J.J.'s building dates from 1910, and although it was built when the Liberty style was in full flow, it is actually in the Gothic Revival style of the 19th century. 'It looks like a castle in brick and stone,' explains J.J. 'In the apartment itself everything was handmade by artisans. All the mouldings are incredible. The doors all divide, and there is so much character.' She feels that this made the job of designing the interior much easier: 'In this sort of setting the decorating requires less heavy lifting. I am a collaborative creative. Here I already had a theme given to me by the bones of the building that I could then have a visual discourse with.'

J.J.'s friend, the decorative arts dealer Raimondo Garau, who has an amazing eye for furniture, helped her to track down just the right pieces. Although he did not decorate the interior, he was a great sounding board as the spaces evolved, each taking on their own personality. 'There is not a single white wall,' says J.J. 'All the colours were mixed by the painter onsite.' She knew she wanted a dark green for the guest bedroom, which is often occupied by any of her friends or spiritual teachers who happen to be passing through Milan. After trialling self-described 'wimpy' colours at the start, J.J. finally painted her own bedroom a deep burgundy. 'Now I feel like I'm living inside the womb of Mother Earth,' she says. In the living room, a needlepoint tapestry of a unicorn surveys the apartment from one of the walls. 'I collect art and go with visuals that make me excited,' explains J.J. 'The unicorn is a mythical creature and represents magic. One could say it is the spirit animal of the whole house.'

'Every room in my apartment speaks to a different individual,' says J.J. Some love the bathroom, in which all her vintage necklaces are hung on the wall as though in a gallery. Others prefer the dining room, with its impactful wallpaper. 'I was spending a lot of time in Bali,' J.J. explains. 'My boyfriend at the time stumbled upon books there filled with Japanese collages. I took photos and asked my design team to create prints out of them. Although the designs weren't suitable for clothing, I had an artist make me wallpaper instead. I measured all the walls myself and sent her all the measurements. Each wall is framed by colour, and she added my dog Pepper to the design.'

J.J. is a real homebody, and her environment is very important to her. 'It's something I need to curate,' she explains. 'I need to have a wonderful, beautiful container that feels very well structured and organised and visually pleasing. That's how I get my sense of safety. And then I can create from that place. In the end I need an interior that feels inviting, juicy, joyful.'

'I think there are design rules, but I don't know what they are, and I don't follow them... It's not a good idea to create an entire room that's from one period. You really have to mix styles or materials. I like to have different surface textures. I also like symmetry in a room. Symmetry calms the system; it taps into sacred geometry, which is always symmetrical.'

'Everything in Italy takes longer. You're going to need at least a year to figure out what the house needs. Then a second year to get things going. Everything exercises your patience, and you have to accept that.'

JUXTAPOSITION / *I don't know that I design by creating specific 'vignettes'. Also, I don't think anything in my home is truly 'disparate'; even if they're from completely different periods or parts of the world, they are things that evoke something important for me. Customising vintage pieces with some of my favourite La DoubleJ prints does keep a sort of fil rouge running through the space.*

BALANCE / *Editing is a key part of creating a space that flows. Too many microprints can be jarring or overwhelming, but too much blank space can feel stark and sterile. Some of the rooms in my home have wildly patterned wallpaper, whereas others have a different solid colour. Even as a maximalist, I can appreciate that there must be some negative space if the eye is to have room to settle.*

SURPRISE / *Perhaps the fact that every individual room has its own personality.*

COLOUR / *Colour has its own energetic frequency that can be imprinted upon us as humans, so it's vitally important to me. (It's one of the reasons we at La DoubleJ create such colourful, wildly printed pieces – they spark joy.)*

PATTERN / *Balance is key. In my dining room, for example, there's a lot going on with the walls, so I like to keep the table fairly minimal. The plain-painted rooms allow me to get more playful with patterned elements, such as cushions, vases or upholstered chairs. The printed rooms in my home have custom-made wallpaper. My bathroom has a La DoubleJ print and my dining room a custom-painted wallpaper by Kirsten Synge, based on the collages found in Bali.*

TEXTURE / *Layering textures has to be about balance. My dining room has an intricate wallpaper, an oversized blue rattan Emmanuelle chair, a vintage Murano glass chandelier, and then a very simple square white Molteni office desk that I use as a dining table. It's a textural playground.*

MOOD / *My home is my sanctuary. I designed it specifically to make me feel good, to inspire my creativity, to be both unique and inviting.*

LIMITATIONS & POSSIBILITIES / *There was not a single light in the apartment. You have to completely create a lighting system in an Italian interior, and that can require a lot of work. I have many interesting light sources in the apartment, and although some rooms don't have enough light, I prefer to have moody lighting – it makes things more romantic. Another challenge in Italian houses is that there is no storage. In particular, there are no closets in most buildings, and no built-in kitchens. I took a whole Poggenpohl kitchen from another apartment across town and had it reinstalled here. The price of reusing a vintage kitchen was less than the Ikea one I had budgeted for.*

ALL THINGS CONSIDERED / *My home, just like me, is constantly evolving. It's like a map of where I've been, what's affected me most, and what's stirring my imagination in the moment.*

GERT VOORJANS

The interior architect Gert Voorjans inhabits a 19th-century mansion in the centre of Antwerp, a city known for its intermingling of history, cutting-edge creativity and commerce. Walking around Gert's neighbourhood in the theatre district, one feels that idyllic balance of a village in town, with artistic vitality, ordered terraces, small stores and authentic flower shops. The main façade and distinctive Art Deco windows of the building – which was transformed in the 1930s by the interbellum architect Joseph Selis – overlook an attractive square. But this ordered 20th-century frontage conceals unexpected and charming historic rooms.

Born into a family of furniture traders and carpenters, Gert grew up surrounded by beautiful landscape. His early career involved spending time in Siena, London and various parts of Japan, and he also gained a covetable commission from the fashion designer Dries Van Noten to design his brand's retail outlets worldwide and even the designer's private castle in the Belgian countryside.

Gert's own house contains his private rooms and professional spaces, with the ground and first floors set aside for Gert Voorjans Studio and the upper levels an intimate residence. Walking up from street level, the experience is of a playful yet knowledgeable approach to decoration that combines styles and periods. 'I like the best of different worlds', Gert says in his warm, welcoming voice. 'When imagining a room, there is not always one solution. I study and look at the past to understand the future. My aim is to create fresh, modern interiors that are forward-looking. I pick different periods without staying in any single one. My style involves not only assembling things but also combining them in an exciting way. I believe in personal style in my projects, and there is always something of me in my rooms. I take things that appeal to me and make them new while they are in my care.'

Architecturally trained, Gert has the passion of a curator, which he deploys to craft layered rooms with great depth. At home he uses different spaces depending on the season, and the layout never remains static. 'I am attracted to light and beautiful windows,' he explains. 'I sit close to the windows in summer and in front of the open fire in winter. The position of furniture is not fixed, and I often move it around to suit the time of year. I bring in fresh flowers and nice plants. I cannot stand a place to be immobile – that is not interesting. You must put energy into a room, [and you can do this] by bringing in colour. Every room can be attractive, but it must [be able to] adapt.'

Given some of the striking decorating gestures in Gert's home, guests are often surprised by how cosy it is, and by the kindness of the approach to interior design. 'Artists' studios – which develop organically – are my all-time inspiration. In the salon, I want to give that energy to [the visitor] from the moment they walk in.' Objects are placed on unexpected perches: a statue on a ladder, or by the sofa a rubber plant so large that one imagines sitting under a great tree in a forest. 'I follow my instinct to imagine rooms for my own pleasure,' Gert says, 'not just following a scheme.'

'We are lucky,' Gert says, 'still to have beautiful old houses with high ceilings and good proportions that bring poetry into an interior. My dream as a child was to live in a house with wooden floors, high ceilings and an open fire.' He now lives in that and much more. In his meticulously orchestrated spatial arrangements, he accomplishes more than merely arranging beautiful objects and furniture; he infuses his interiors with grace and fluidity, meaning and appropriateness that are increasingly rare.

'I believe in Colour, Character and Craftsmanship, and that is also the manifesto of my office. Colour means you have verve. I don't do mainstream; I'm always looking for a more interesting, characterful solution. A library can be in a staircase, for example. That's why people consult me. I have to be creative. And I always work with local craftspeople whenever possible. I want to fight for authenticity.'

'At home I want to create a
symphony that works with
glamour, impact and style.
When I create a space, I think
about the possibilities
and stop being limited.
I don't like matching suites.
Nor am I fond of too much
of one style. I like to play
and create a context that is
friendly and fresh.'

JUXTAPOSITION / *I like de-proportions, the contrast of proportions to keep the attention of a viewer. The eye has to travel across a room, and I achieve this through visual dialogue, interaction and contrast, such as a huge vase.*

BALANCE / *Balance comes from harmony through diversion. I love a huge tapestry, then a table in front with smaller objects. One wall of my living room is covered in something, while another is completely empty. It gives the interior room to breathe, and you can discover something interesting in that context. I'm fond of sculpture in the living room. Some elements must be extraordinary to balance a space.*

SURPRISE / *I am keen on large, extravagant fireplaces, with a nod to humour. The fireplace is an important item – when you can have one. We are all so sophisticated these days, but what is nicer than that connection to nature in a world that has become so artificial?*

COLOUR / *Colour, for me, is a structural element that I can build on or which can be a backbone for the rest of the interior. It's like construction. I think in colour; I look through the home and create a colour palette for the setting with a sense of place. At home I'm very playful. Colour is about framing – supporting what you bring in.*

PATTERN / *I love pattern, but I also like to create pattern by using a lot of plains. I don't do many patterns in every room. There must be a balance. For me, the ceiling of the guest bedroom, which came from the Moroccan pavilion at the 1958 world exhibition in Brussels, is an object. Pattern can also be created by the objects you choose.*

TEXTURE / *I strongly believe in bringing tactility to interiors. I love the touch of silk in combination with cotton and velvet, for example. I like materials that age well. It's wonderful to touch a beautiful table with a surface that has acquired a patina over time.*

MOOD / *The mood is poetry based on Colour, Character and Craftsmanship.*

LIMITATIONS & POSSIBILITIES / *What seems to be a limitation at the beginning of the process will often be the saviour of authenticity. I have no garden, but that makes me go out. I don't have a lift, but that makes me exercise. When it comes to creating options in a space, I work around the problems and explore different possibilities for the floorplan. You come to solutions by being creative. My breakfast table, for example, is almost in the staircase. I like to use corridors and landings when possible, since these spaces are relaxed and unpredictable.*

ALL THINGS CONSIDERED / *It's unconventional, it's a homely home.*

RODMAN PRIMACK
& RUDY WEISSENBERG

Lomas de Chapultepec, Mexico City

Interior designers and gallerists Rodman Primack and Rudy Weissenberg are partners in both life and work. The warmth and big-heartedness of this approachable couple perhaps explain their dynamic careers.

Rodman has spent many years in leadership positions in the world of art and design as well as founding the interior-design practice RP Miller, now AGO Interiors. Rudy was a media executive before pursuing his passion for design, which led him to curate shows in London and New York. In 2019 Rodman (originally from California) and Rudy (born in Guatemala) founded AGO Projects, the acclaimed gallery for contemporary collectible design, joined by their studio AGO Interiors, and the two now work together across all projects.

Their nomadic lives have led them to Mexico, a country known for its vibrancy and creative energy, and one they always told friends they would move to. 'Our neighbourhood is in one of the "fancy" parts of town, but that is not why we live there. It's hilly, green and leafy, and in a city with frequent earthquakes, it is great that it is on bedrock (much of the city is on a sandy lakebed). Las Lomas [de Chapultepec] is sort of like the Upper East Side of Mexico City. Something else we love about it is that you really only hear Spanish spoken there.' The couple live in Las Lomas for their specific building, which dates from 1952 and was designed by the great Mexican modernist architect Augusto H. Alvarez, who was influenced by the International Style of Le Corbusier and Ludwig Mies van der Rohe.

Rodman fell in love with the building on his first visit . A former colleague from Christie's who lived there – and still does – raved about it. 'We love mid-century modernist buildings,' says Rodman, 'and this is a perfect example, surrounded by big old trees and a garden. It's a little oasis in a busy city.'

The couple's style is driven by their desire to collect things, to live with art and objects, to entertain casually and frequently, and to focus on enjoying life in their space. 'We love colour, clearly, and pattern too,' says Rudy. 'Minimalism is so beautiful, but it doesn't work for us because we love too many things and want to live with them. We design to maximise utility and pleasure, and for us that means an interior that is not complicated or precious, one where we can receive friends, guests or groups, or be at home by ourselves with our rescue dog Chapo and feel cosy.'

An accomplished cook, Rodman spends a lot of time in the kitchen, which has an incredible view and lots of indirect light. 'The yellow is so cheerful in the morning,' he says, although as a generous host he enjoys preparing food there at all times. Really, though, he loves to sit in the office, reading and working at the desk that belonged to Rudy's grandfather. The enveloping green is very calming and helps him to focus. Rudy loves reading in bed.

Friends love the apartment because it is so personal. 'It may not be for everyone,' says Rodman, 'but it is very clearly us, so I think people immediately feel comfortable because we are so comfortable [there]. People often comment on the different objects and artworks, the vintage and contemporary furniture.' The main ingredient in the scheme was love, the couple say candidly: 'It's so lame but it's true: everything in that apartment is loved, and nothing is dispensable.'

'The moment we see rules, we think of how to work around them or prove them wrong. Our only rule today is not to be competitive with social media or [photos in] magazines, to focus on what is truly important to you and your life and how you live it. If you don't entertain, don't have a dining room that seats 24!'

'Nothing is flatter than a simply pretty-on-pretty-on-pretty room. "Ugly" things are important and can put the beautiful in relief, otherwise it all becomes like a one-note song. Snore.'

RODMAN PRIMACK & RUDY WEISSENBERG / **87**

JUXTAPOSITION / *The starting point for us is the fact that we always have so much stuff we want to look at. Our groupings come out of the desire/need to see things, to not keep them in storage – not to make vignettes, even though those are pleasing.*

BALANCE / *We move and change things all the time. This is less true of paintings or things on the wall, but we do edit and add and tinker. Sometimes a little messy is good too, but in general we do like to make stacks and piles and organise. We often live with lots of open shelving, and we tell people that's easy if you don't buy ugly things to begin with.*

SURPRISE / *Our houses never look too stiff or formal because we aren't like that. Our taste is eclectic and would be labelled by others high/low, but we don't see it that way. Everything is of the same value to us, from something picked up in a local market to a gallery-purchased work by a recognised artist. If we like it or find it special, that's all that matters and it's equal.*

COLOUR / *Colour is everything. We love white-on-white interiors, but that has never been our thing [to live in]. We believe colour affects all aspects of your life and how you feel. Colour is super-dependent on location; what works in Mexico isn't necessarily going to work in London, and there are qualities of colours that just don't work in the same way.*

PATTERN / *We love mixed patterns, but we think it's all about finding balance between scale of print, intensity of colour and saturation, density of pattern, and so on. We have mixed antique Japanese handblocked prints with vintage waxed English chintz and Indonesian batik and American cotton quilts – and it has worked. In our minds, there are no rules when it comes to pattern.*

TEXTURE / *We usually veer towards simple finishes: paint or fabric on walls, simple plaster. We think about how walls absorb or reflect light and how that affects art, objects and fabrics in the room. We love the word 'negative' in this context, meaning that a colour or texture acts as a negative, absorbing light.*

MOOD / *In Mexico the mood is mellow and warm, and we want everyone to feel comfortable and at home with us. The low vintage Scarpa sofas (which belonged to Rudy's grandparents) help the whole thing to feel relaxed and anti-stiff. We don't give too much importance to anything, even when it is 'important'.*

LIMITATIONS & POSSIBILITIES / *Limitations and constraints are what make good projects. Having to push up against structure and so on is what forces good ideas and resolutions. The worst projects we have seen are [those where the designer had] carte blanche with zero limitations. We hate to say it, but the best work we have seen, especially in architecture, is the moment when some money comes out of a project and solutions emerge!*

ALL THINGS CONSIDERED / *We like that it is so clearly ours. It is unmistakably Rodman and Rudy, and exactly what we need and want. What a privilege that is.*

RODMAN PRIMACK & RUDY WEISSENBERG / **89**

TIMOTHY CORRIGAN

16ième, Paris

This welcoming apartment in the 16th arrondissement has enviable views across an elegant, quiet residential neighbourhood to the Eiffel Tower. Inhabited by Timothy Corrigan – principal of Timothy Corrigan, Inc., an in-demand residential design firm with offices in Los Angeles and Paris – the interior thoughtfully mixes periods and one-of-a-kind objects discovered at auctions and the Paris flea market. Timothy first moved to Paris more than 30 years ago to work for a large advertising agency, and it was love at first sight.

Built to impress, the building was designed at the height of the Belle Époque, an era when socialising and keeping up appearances were competitive sports. In most Parisian apartment buildings that date from the city's mid-19th-century renovation masterminded by Georges-Eugène Haussmann, with a single apartment per floor, the second and fifth floors are the prime apartments. Here, however, it is the second and fourth floors that are the most covetable, being beautifully detailed and with higher ceilings than those on the other levels. Timothy's apartment is on the fourth floor, and from the bones of the architecture it is clear that he picked the right one. He uses it for his monthly trips to Paris, when he visits his current design projects, and as a pit stop before heading to his country house, Château de la Chevallarie, in the northern Loire Valley.

Once guests get over the wow factor of the entrance hall, with its inlaid French cabinet on a stand, large mismatched octagonal 1960s and theatrical 1940s mirrors and confidently positioned Matisse lithograph terminating the vista, they soon relax. 'I've focused on comfortable elegance,' Timothy explains, 'which simply means that I don't believe in sacrificing liveability to achieve a specific look. If a room isn't comfortable, no matter how beautifully it might be decorated, to me, it's not successful. And comfort is more than just the way a chair feels when you sit down – it is also a state of mind, the assurance that you can be yourself in a space and do as you please, such as feeling at ease [enough] to put your feet up on a coffee table.' Inspired by the comfort of an English country house, but working in a chic Parisian building, he left room for large, inviting upholstered seating as well as dramatic touches, such as the pair of larger-than-life 1920s plaster statues that guard the living room.

Timothy's study, a moodier space across the hall, transports you to the pages of a French novel, such is the powerful sense of place. 'I love this room, which was originally the apartment's dining room,' he says. 'It has a wonderful beamed ceiling that I painted green and enhanced with decorative motifs drawn from a French Directoire-style wallpaper by the London firm Iksel.'

Walking around the 325-sq-m (3,500-sq-ft) apartment, one feels that each room was created with a very strong idea about the way it would be used, whether for an evening cocktail party, relaxing on a sunny day with light streaming through the windows or dinner with friends. 'Despite the sophisticated elegance, people are always surprised at how warm my home feels,' Timothy says. 'They also love to look at the architectural detailing, which has been highlighted with multiple shades of paint.' By not sticking to the conventional intended use for each room, Timothy has made each space special. The large dining room having become an office, a dark guest room was transformed into an intimate dining room that is light-filled during the day but at night glows by warm candlelight. How very Parisian!

'I'm a maximalist, and all my homes have a mix of furniture, art and accessories that I've collected over the years. I'm never quite done, adding more, swapping things out or moving them around. My interiors are a work in progress – just like me.'

'I incorporate original art
and antiques into all my
projects. They introduce
history and soul to any
space. Art doesn't have to
be of the highest quality,
but it is very important to
surround yourself with
pieces that make you smile.'

JUXTAPOSITION / *I combine items that are similar, yet distinct. For example, I wanted to create an interesting tension between the two living rooms, to reiterate their connection but subtly undercut any expectation that they are the same – much as the architecture, with its slight variations, does. The mantels match, but the overmantel mirrors don't; both rooms feature Baccarat crystal chandeliers, but they are not identical – brother and sister, rather than twins. Both rooms contain watercolours by Auguste Rodin. Between the windows of the evening room is a portrait of Louis XV, while a bust of him oversees a corner of the daytime room.*

BALANCE / *I prefer rooms that are accessorised and look lived in. I place objects symmetrically or use pairs, which helps to prevent them from looking messy or too busy.*

SURPRISE / *I mix periods and styles, and find one-of-a-kind objects at auctions and the Paris flea market. I particularly like pairing things of vastly different quality, because it helps you to appreciate each for its inherent design value, regardless of the cost.*

COLOUR / *My former flat in Paris used much cooler, crisp colours, so I intentionally went warmer here, with lights in shades of cream and green. I linked the study to the adjacent hall and the salons by using the same sunny yellow colour, but here in reverse, as a background that highlights the white centre panels, which are outlined in green. I love the way the warm tones feel very inviting and bring a cosy feeling to the more formal pieces of art and furniture.*

PATTERN / *I typically use solid colours or subtle patterns on large pieces of furniture, and stronger patterns on the supporting players. I try not to repeat patterns, such as stripes, in the same space, and [instead] tie them together by colour.*

TEXTURE / *Mixing textures is vital to creating a vibrant space. This is especially true when decorating with a neutral palette. It can be achieved by pairing plush fabrics with a wooden coffee table, topped with stone or metal objects, a crystal chandelier and a gilt-wood mirror. Inviting everyone to the party makes any space more interesting.*

MOOD / *Each room has a different mood, which is achieved by colour, pattern and furniture styles. For example, the small salon feels bright and casual, from the selection of my light-coloured 'Go for Baroque' pattern for Perennials outdoor fabrics on the chairs, while the large salon feels richer because of the moss-green silk velvet on the sofas.*

LIMITATIONS & POSSIBILITIES / *This flat is palatial by Parisian standards, so there weren't many design restrictions but, with creativity and ingenuity, there's always a solution to restrictions or limitations. Sometimes you must embrace the imperfections and realise that they give quirky character to a space.*

ALL THINGS CONSIDERED / *What I like most about my home is that it serves my needs for the way I want to live. I encourage everyone to break some rules and live with the confidence that your home is your castle, no matter the size or place.*

MICHAL SILVER /
Chelsea, London

Born in Israel, the designer Michal Silver lived a rather nomadic life between Tel Aviv, New York and Paris before settling in London 28 years ago. Having studied fine arts and had a career as a fashion designer, she is currently creative director at Christopher Farr Cloth. This respected London brand is known for producing and designing bold textiles, wallpapers and trims, often through exciting creative collaborations with resident artists and archival collections.

Michal's building is near Brompton Cemetery, in a conservation area at the far western end of Chelsea, on the border with Fulham. This is the Chelsea that was once a haven for artists, musicians and later the punk movement. There is a young vibe in the neighbourhood, with busy streets, gorgeous buildings from different periods, small yet exquisite gardens. Originally part of a Congregational chapel built in 1855, her home feels peaceful, and inside the noise of the city disappears.

'As soon as I walked in two years ago, I knew this was it,' says Michal. 'I fell in love with the emptiness and the large open-centre hall, which allowed for a sitting area, a reading corner, an eating space and a kitchen. There was no fussiness in the pared-down structure, and I adored that skeletal anatomy of the space.' The architecture creates a framework for the interiors, like a frame for an artwork, yet is also functional and structural, setting the tone for the way the house was decorated. It is now home to Michal, her husband and their two daughters.

This atypical Chelsea home certainly offers a wow effect. Entry is through a small hallway that opens up to a single large, soaring, uninterrupted room, grand and unexpected in this neighbourhood known for its narrow townhouses. Stylish yet somewhat monastic, it offers a place of repose for a designer who is surrounded by colour and pattern all day long. 'I work for a company where colour is at the heart of who we are,' explains Michal. 'Coming home, I need to move away from it slightly to a space where there is serenity.' The interiors are not too conscientious, and there is a lot of deliberate empty space. It's a refuge.

There are a few pieces of furniture and artworks that the couple have acquired over the years: an Alvar Aalto chair, for example, an Eames Elliptical coffee table and a Ron Arad 'Victoria & Albert' sofa for Moroso. 'I love my two Sandra Blow collages from her (very short-lived) "Matisse" period, for their scale and exuberant colour. I am very familiar with her work and a huge admirer, and we collaborated on a wall-covering collection for Cloth.' Michal adores the reading corner, where she feels completely in her element. She lounges on the most comfortable chair, the 'Wink' by Toshiyuki Kita, next to a jolly mid-century three-arm floor lamp with conical shades in primary colours. 'We created corners that frame the space without having to divide it or put in partitions,' she says. 'There is a flow, and you meander into areas and have your own cocoons. Being to the left of the main door, the reading area is a bit hidden.'

Michal finds it difficult to speak about inspiration, since the house reflects the family's lifestyle, journey and travels: 'It has developed, it has evolved, and it has come together over the years because one has pieces gathered over time and from other homes. Adding and taking out, I am surrounded by things I love. We get attached to art and furniture. These are the things I like to have next to me, like pieces of jewellery that you keep.'

'When thinking about my home, I think of the people who live in it every day and the friends who join us for dinner, stay and make the space alive. A good house ages well if you are gentle and considered with the changes you make.'

'It's a very fine line between when something works and when it doesn't. It's like walking on a rope – you just have to try and try again. I suspect time is a good way to judge. You live in a space and one day you just know whether something is right or not.'

JUXTAPOSITION / *Start with two or three good pieces. They can be art, furniture, a rug or even an unusual object. I see interiors as evolving; you make changes as life unfolds, but most importantly you do not have to get it right from the start.*

BALANCE / *There is no mess in my surroundings, since I am a minimalist. The phrase 'less is more' is very reflective of my lifestyle, whether it's the way I dress or a dinner party where there is abundant food but not so much that all the flavours blend.*

SURPRISE / *In our textile collection, as in my home, we don't follow trends. We have a cohesive story that is refined through every launch, and in my house, changes happen with the acquisition of a new piece. I am never in a rush to make the house look perfect. It's an evolution.*

COLOUR / *Colour has a way of transforming a space. I dress with colour and pattern, but at home it's much more of a Zen environment and colour is present through art, a red stairwell and a green patio, which is an extension of the living area. For the patio I wanted green to bring the outside in, and it was next to the Sandra Blow painting, so I wanted to connect the two.*

PATTERN / *The living area is defined by two 'historical' rugs produced by Christopher Farr: in the reading corner, 'Equator' by the celebrated Italian fashion designer Romeo Gigli, an explosion of strokes of red; and, in the sitting area, a '447' rug by the textile artist Gunta Stölzl, the only female master in the Bauhaus. This is a very Bauhausian juxtaposition of geometric patterns in primary colours.*

TEXTURE / *I never have a plan. For me, looking at texture is intuitive, but it's always about comfort over a specific look. I have layered fabrics ranging from the loose cotton cover on the red butterfly chair to the 'Bolton' boucle in Ecru by Christopher Farr Cloth on the 'Gogan' sofa by Italian brand Moroso, and a worn-out leather sofa. Textures have a huge presence and can make a room feel eclectic, tailored or capture the essence of a certain period.*

MOOD / *Harmonious, I would say, putting different elements together, with different references, different historical periods, to create a connection that works. Colours bring a feeling of elegance but not fussiness.*

LIMITATIONS & POSSIBILITIES / *It's imperative to listen to a space and take the time to live in it. For example, experiencing the way the light changes allows you to make the room work. There is no sense of urgency to complete a home in one go. When we moved in two years ago, we had our furniture and artwork and gently fitted them in. Then, gradually, we changed the dining-room table and chairs, as well as the two rugs that grounded the furniture with the dark oak floors. With me, things happen in a very gentle way.*

ALL THINGS CONSIDERED / *There are so many things I love about my home. I love the unconventional structure, the fact that it's an old chapel and has that lofty feel. I love the way the eye can travel in the space.*

PATRICK WILLIAMS & NERIMAN KAMCILI / *Bath, Somerset*

The popular Bath design shop Berdoulat shares its name with an 18th-century farmhouse in south-western France, the childhood home of its founder, the interior designer Patrick Williams. His parents bought the French house as a ruin when he was in the womb, and restored it gradually over 20 years. The thought and processes involved in this venture rubbed off on Patrick as he grew up, and he developed a passion for buildings, furniture, objects and decoration.

Patrick's current home occupies the floors above and rooms behind the shop in a charming and generously proportioned Grade II listed building in a quiet neighbourhood within reach of the centre of this Georgian city. There is a lively community of fellow independent shopkeepers in the area, and a genteel buzz in the air. Patrick's building is 1760s at the front, 1840s in the middle and 1800 at the rear, with sympathetic additions by him and his Bulgarian-born wife Neri, who runs the shop. 'As a designer I loved the combination of 18th- and 19th-century elements, as well as the blend between commercial and domestic,' he says. 'Previously we lived in an 18th-century Bath townhouse – a beautiful building, but one which dictates fairly strictly what one can do with it, whereas here, the differing eras and uses of the building provide a much wider blank canvas. Neri, our two daughters, Wren and Bonnie, and two doggies, Moon and Elizabeth, and I share the house and care for this special building.'

A response to the host building, the interior style could be described as 'classic', devoid of any trend. The new extension, which elegantly rationalises the house's floorplan and blends with the different historical layers, looks as though it has always been there. A library and music space, it contains a virginal and busts of each member of the family made by sculptor friend Claire Loder, various rugs from trips to Istanbul and further afield, and paintings by Patrick's mother. The family dedicated this light-filled space at the heart of the building to Patrick's mother, who died during the build, and it is known in her honour as the 'Rosie Room'. The gold letters painted above the bookcase spell out her name, and her painter's palette is placed casually – almost incidentally – on a shelf.

Although it has a door that connects directly to the shop, the room feels serene. It links both laterally and vertically the various elements of family life, from cooking and eating to relaxing by the fire, providing connections to the kids' bedrooms and the first-floor roof terrace. 'Many enjoy how various the spaces are, each with its own character,' explains Patrick. 'Many feel rather lost, initially, as it's rather a warren of rooms!'

There is a single colour scheme throughout the ground and first floors, a combination of blues and browns, while on the second floor it's a mix of greens. Having been approached by the paint manufacturer Farrow & Ball to collaborate on a colour while the extension was being built, Patrick and Neri knew exactly what they wanted to recreate. 'What's now known as "Berdoulat Green" is copied from the inside of a cupboard upstairs,' says Patrick, 'where the original Georgian paint remained. We sent off the cupboard door to Farrow & Ball's HQ in Wimborne, where the original arsenic-based green pigment was expertly matched.'

In his work as a designer, Patrick abides by the notion that the building is the client. As such, the design of any architectural details and interiors – including those in his home – is a direct response to the host building, its history, its fabric, its setting and its spirit. In his interior, Patrick has achieved a respectful mix. For him, the most important element in design is honesty: 'Whatever is introduced, or whatever work carried out, must be in harmony with, and the correct approach for, the host building. If using reclaimed ingredients, they should be seamlessly introduced, and any newly made elements should use techniques and materials that are sympathetic.'

'The building is the boss – and as such should dictate what's done to it and how. I never break that rule, and I feel that if you follow it, you can't go too wrong with design decisions.'

'It's essential not to try too hard. Successful spaces feel as though they've always been there or have come together organically over time. Nothing should be too considered or relate to any trend. Often, it's a case of the simpler the better!'

JUXTAPOSITION / *The best are the result of chance. Interiors are portraits of the people who inhabit them. One's journey through life is inevitably unpredictable, governed by chance and fate, love and death. I feel the best interiors are a reflection of this random pattern.*

BALANCE / *It's sometimes tricky, when one loves collecting things, to house them in a way that doesn't look chaotic. I love the English country-garden approach, whereby there are strong compartments (a meaningful shelf …) that house an explosion of form and colour (riddled with plaster casts and dripping with plants). I think if one contains collections of objects in this way, surrounded by sparse space, the overall room will look less messy.*

SURPRISE / *I never try too hard to generate a 'look' or 'feel'. I prefer to allow spaces to come together organically over time. Of course, there is a little curating in so doing, but it feels more as though the objects and the building call the shots in terms of what fits where and why. This results in surprise juxtapositions, and sometimes humorous ones.*

COLOUR / *I am becoming increasingly confident in the use of strong colour, having previously been rather terrified of it. I like to keep walls and ceilings light on the whole (I love bare lime plaster finishes with clear beeswax atop), then introduce colour via woodwork.*

PATTERN / *The mixture of patterns is not intentional, but the result of accidental juxtapositions.*

TEXTURE / *Ditto. Equally accidental.*

MOOD / *Each room has a totally different mood, and I love that about our home. I've never tried to assign a mood to a space, as I think mood is something inherent in the bones of a building. The way in which light behaves, the acoustics, even the smell can dictate a feeling. For me, it's more a passive appreciation for these elements in our home, than an intended blend.*

LIMITATIONS & POSSIBILITIES / *Our designs had to factor in listed-building consent, which, one could argue, is always restrictive. However, all the works we proposed were ultimately beneficial to the preservation of the fabric of the building, and where any new fabric was introduced, we were extremely careful not to be disruptive. When adding structural steels to carry the extension above the kitchen, for example, we had to work closely with the structural engineer to ensure that they were as subtle as possible. We managed to hide pretty much all of them and disrupted none of the original fabric of the building during the installation, which was quite a feat.*

ALL THINGS CONSIDERED / *I enjoy how the open-plan living on the ground and first floors is both lateral and vertical (with the various stairways and first-floor rooms giving on to the galleried section of the double-height ground-floor kitchen). This allows each member of the family to have their own space and do their own thing, while simultaneously being connected.*

HOLLY HOWE

Dartmouth Park, London

'I've lived all around London, but I've never felt as at home as I do in Dartmouth Park,' says Holly Howe (an interior designer and co-creative director at British brand Howe London) of the leafy area bordering the south-eastern corner of Hampstead Heath. 'It's a countryside bubble in the heart of the city, green and wild with a brilliant sense of community, full of interesting, creative residents who all seem to have deep roots in the area.'

Holly, her husband, their two little boys (aged one and five) and their Maltipoo dog, Bear, live in a wonderfully wonky Victorian end-of-terrace house. The fact that it is an end-of-terrace property grants it an extra wedge of space, so every floor feels bigger than you'd expect. Before Holly and her family moved in, it had last been renovated – although not very well – in the 1980s. 'The fireplaces needed reinstating and the cornicing restoring,' she recalls, 'but the bones and the light were just perfect. It's one of those special little streets where properties don't come up much because it's tucked away and there's such a fantastic sense of community.'

Holly grew up with very creative parents, who became antique dealers without meaning to. From the moment she was born, the family's home was constantly evolving, a veritable treasure trove of antique furniture and objects coming and going. 'Howe London (and the style synonymous with Howe London and my dad) is part of my DNA, so much of my own taste has grown from those roots, expressed through a disregard of trends and fashion, favouring honesty, quality and charm as well as an unintentional obsession with collecting!'

Holly loves waking up in her bedroom, a favourite space, to the optimistic 'Pondicherry' wallpaper from the family's textile business, 36 Bourne Street. 'It's a pattern rather than a solid that's easy live with,' she explains, 'a diagonal pattern with a subtle linear shape, used in an oddly shaped room.' The natural linen curtains lined with vintage mattress fabric bring calm to the room, and on sunny days light plays through them, revealing the charming stripes of the lining. 'We upgraded to a super-king bed when we moved here,' Holly says, 'so in the morning the kids and the dog all pile in with us and we start the day there together.' Referring to the bed covered in cushions, she adds, 'we have a Swedish friend who comes to London with amazing deliveries of Swedish cushions. It's hard to resist their lovely informality. I love the mix of stripes, and the extra cushions add comfort.'

Although the family has lived in the house for only three years, it feels established, as if they have been there a long time. Holly didn't use a moodboard or scheme when creating her interior, and she hasn't referenced other interiors or periods specifically: 'I'm quite sentimental, so there are certain pieces (objects and furniture) that I'm very attached to or that make me feel happy, and I think these subconsciously became the starting point for the house.' Wandering around the spaces, there's a wonderful mid-century Swedish handwoven 'Flossa' carpet on the wall of the family room. A gift from her dad (and their great friend Bjarne) some years before she moved to this house, and once stored away because she had nowhere to display it, it has now found a home in Dartmouth Park. Her set of original Ernest Race dining chairs and other treasures have comfortably settled, framed by the wallpapers from 36 Bourne Street that Holly had been dying to use for herself. All these elements blend to create a relaxed atmosphere in which everyone has a chance to feel at ease and at home.

'I didn't have any time to plan ahead. Work was busy, Bertie (my elder son) was two and the builders were ready to go, so I had to keep up with their schedule: 'We need the skirting this week, what colour would you like this room?' I was always a little behind.'

'I like being surrounded by pieces that have had a life before me and that will last beyond me. [I like it] from a sustainability perspective, but also, I think, because it has a stabilising, calming effect on an interior. People and their interiors will come and go, but these things will still be there … somewhere.'

JUXTAPOSITION / *It's helpful to have a common thread, no matter how tenuous.*
We live in such a green area of London, that the colour and nature became a web that spun through
the house, from the green walls and pictures in the study to the waney edged oak kitchen worktop
and the kids' many treasured collections of sticks and stones.

BALANCE / *Symmetry is best avoided, it's a very simplistic approach to achieving balance,*
which – as nature teaches us – is far more complicated than it looks.

SURPRISE / *Growing up, I don't think we ever had a home that was really 'finished'.*
My home now is the closest I've come to that; the building work is complete (thank goodness),
but the idea of being finished feels impossibly stiff, claustrophobic even. With two little boys,
a 650-sq-m (7,000-sq-ft) warehouse full of ever-changing pieces and an inherited addiction
to antiques markets, our life and home will never stop evolving.

COLOUR / *Gaining space when we moved felt very liberating. Each room could have*
its own identity and its own colour, so I could have much more fun! I didn't really think in terms
of colour palette, my choices were more instinctive, but reading them all together now there
is an optimism and light-heartedness that unite the colours.

PATTERN / *Things don't have to match, but colour does unite elements.*
Pattern is very good for a lifestyle that involves children and dogs. You can have fun with it,
and its main intention can be practicality. I find it much easier to combine and overlay vintage
patterns and textiles, or new patterns that are woven and developed in the same way as the antique
references. This is mainly because the quality of colour and base cloth/material is just so much
better than most modern textiles, so you get a wonderful, varied depth of colour and
pattern that naturally wears better over time, too.

TEXTURE / *When you look at fabrics and make decisions in the space, it leads to better*
outcomes. I had already lived in my bedroom when I chose the curtains, so I was aware of the light.
They are not blackout curtains, and you get a mottled effect from the linen lined with stripes.

MOOD / *Happy! Achieved by choosing things not for 'a look'*
but that I (and we as a family) love and enjoy.

LIMITATIONS & POSSIBILITIES / *My choices were limited in some ways by having*
two very small children. Good quality gloss-painted surfaces come into their own and well-made
furniture can withstand a few years of little climbers, but certainly I had to think 'robust, durable,
won't show stains'. Seeing the amazing antiques that come through Howe, I have learned a thing
or two about what materials can endure and how they wear.

ALL THINGS CONSIDERED / *I get a lot of joy from seeing how relaxed and happy*
people feel in the house. There is so much variation and so much to see. It just works very well,
and we use it fully. It is the way we want it, and the spaces will evolve as the family changes.
We have created a context for our family to live in over the years.

HOLLY HOWE / **157**

ANTHONY COLLETT

Shepherd's Bush, London

Born in British Northern Rhodesia (now Zambia) and schooled in South Africa, the interior architect and designer Anthony Collett lives in a thriving multiracial neighbourhood in west London. 'We are close to one of the oldest open street markets in the city,' he explains, 'where there are traditional English sellers, Polish and Asian vendors and Middle Eastern stalls. There is always something interesting. I'm thrilled that there are wonderful foods, people and a stimulating effervescence in the community. Perhaps this keeps me close to my origins in Africa.'

The Victorian townhouse, now brimming with flair and connoisseurship, was a clean slate for Anthony to work on. It had never been interfered with, and since the 19th century had been only repaired. 'I didn't have to contend with someone else's refurbishing. I have been the surgeon who has done a facelift on a face that had never been touched. My wife and I live here at present, but it was previously a family home with three children and two dogs, and regularly welcomes our grandchildren.'

Anthony's professional practice is holistic, embracing every aspect of architectural, interior furniture and landscape design, down to the smallest detail. He is known for creating stylish custom-made spaces with a great sense of both order and comfort. At home, however, he is more free and experimental. 'In terms of its architecture, the house was laid out as one idea,' he explains. 'The geography of the rooms is considered, planned and established. The furnishings, however, have evolved through my experimentation. I would not experiment on a client, but I can experiment on myself.'

Anthony has assembled objects that interest him and mixed them in intriguing ways. In the living room, for example, furniture made from buffalo horn sits next to a piece made of forged metal, creating harmony and unexpected visual dialogue. 'The objects I collect live in harmony, even though they are different,' he says. 'I've also learned from the pieces I've collected; the ceramics, particularly, are a lesson in colour. With my architectural background I didn't engage with colour so much, but my ceramics gave me confidence [in that respect],' he adds, referring to an astounding collection of Arts and Crafts ceramics with magnificent glazes.

The kitchen on the lower ground floor is entered via a staircase with fantastical yellow-painted walls by South African artist Nicholaas Maritz. This room is a favourite space, since Anthony loves to entertain and cook. 'What prompted the kitchen's design was that I went to an auction, where I came across enormous oak and Douglas fir cabinets that had come from a church vestry. I bought a big assortment of cabinetry, doors and stained-glass windows, reconfigured them, and used 80 per cent of this find to do the kitchen and dining room. The cabinet that accommodates the sink was designed to hang with the other pieces. It's a complexly panelled wooden room.'

Visitors have referred to the house as a museum, since they tend to see only the reception areas. Yet it is very friendly and cosy. At the same time, the interior is a masterful assemblage of pieces that Anthony has designed in conjunction with furniture that has caught his eye and inspired him. All the art is by people he knows, including the Gilbert and George – a wedding present – above the fireplace in the back living room, and the work by the late David Champion in the bathroom. Because all the elements are so personal, the interiors work as a whole. There is also great order among the apparent chaos. 'Architecturally, in terms of the geography of the house, I'm very drawn to order, but I have also indulged in my own home,' says Anthony. 'I like to compose rooms and buildings in an orderly way and like them to be legible. I like there to be asymmetry or incongruity, yet my chaos is very contrived, and controlled.'

'One sets out to create order and symmetry, but from time to time it is necessary to relieve the monotony by creating something offbeat.'

'I'm influenced by the things and people around me, [as well as] my experiences and background. This makes my interior personal.'

'There is a wide range of
periods and cultures in
the objects I collect, from
contemporary art through
Arts and Crafts and the
Aesthetic Movement to
ancient African art and
sculpture. These are objects
that I have always been
attracted to and learned from.'

JUXTAPOSITION / *Interesting vignettes and juxtapositions are created when the objects used are in conversation with one another and not in conflict. No single piece should steal the show; all should be in harmony.*

BALANCE / *All pieces within a composition should act as one.*

SURPRISE / *There is always an element of surprise, but the art is for these surprises to reveal themselves within the whole, rather than shout at the expense of the rest.*

COLOUR / *Colour is very important in my interior. I have always believed that all good colours can live harmoniously with one another. I think that all well-composed colours can work in harmony with each other. I learnt this from my collection of vases where there was a large range of colours, but once I rearranged them, they always 'sang' together in harmony.*

PATTERN / *Patterns should be mixed in a way that allows them to coexist with one another, and should have the same colour palette and vocabulary. When mixing patterns there should always be a common denominator, even if very concealed and subtle, to bring the mix together.*

TEXTURE / *Many of the materials we used at home are natural materials – wood, stone and metal – and they all contribute their own textures and finishes. The materials each have their own characteristics but they share the fact that they are real and natural and so have this ability to work together.*

MOOD / *Context is very important in terms of mood, and each room is different. The mood of my living room is different from that of my bathroom. In the living room I am constantly looking around and enjoying the art and furniture, rediscovering things that have been with me for a long time. It is very rich and stimulating. The way I've done my bathroom, it feels very serene, like a retreat. All the moods in the house can live harmoniously with one another.*

LIMITATIONS & POSSIBILITIES / *One cuts one's cloth according to the space. Restrictions don't exist, but rather are self-imposed because one has preconceptions of what one wants to achieve, rather than having a dialogue with the space.*

ALL THINGS CONSIDERED / *I like the house's evolving spaces, and its familiarity, which has made it a setting for and extension of the family.*

SASHA BIKOFF

West Village, New York City

'My neighbourhood is very charming,' says New York decorator Sasha Bikoff. 'Our street is a winding, tree-lined one in the West Village, [and our house is] in a row of landmarked old townhouses dating back to the 1870s.' With its many pre-war buildings and lovely parks, it feels the most European among memories of old New York. It's not exactly the sort of place where you might expect to find Sasha, a designer whose work has been labelled 'psychedelic' and 'eyepopping' by the design press. Of course, that unexpectedness is very her, and here she lives with her husband and baby son in a house full of surprises.

Sasha's style is bold and imaginative, inspired by the past, nature, art, architecture and film. Often all these inspirations fuse and a distinctive yet cohesive story is written based on various sources. 'I create a new world based on a story that I make up,' she explains. 'Narrative drives a lot of what I do. I consider myself a storyteller. In the townhouse I imagined an eccentric woman living in her home, her husband allowing her to do whatever she wanted. Colour, pattern and print were cast in the storyline to stimulate her baby visually. I wanted it to feel as though this was a house in London's Notting Hill, a little Victorian with a bit of French country and other references from trips to the European continent. I wanted it to be appropriate for an area where artists, fashion designers and creatives live.'

Sasha, who was pregnant at the time, completed this project very quickly and designed a positive space with something to enjoy everywhere you look. 'I used more traditional sort of prints than I normally do,' she says, 'because the house could handle it. The front door is red,' – a nod to the former name of her street, Cherry Lane – 'and red geraniums sprout from the windowboxes,' which remind her of those on the balconies of the Hôtel Plaza Athénée in Paris. 'Friends love my home, and it always surprises. It excites them visually and they are reminded of certain references that spark a conversation about the house. As you go up the townhouse floors the interiors change, as do the references, yet it all works together.' On the ground floor, a Le Manach wallpaper with a French country vibe mixes with an antique Persian rug with nods to the space age and mid-century styles. Her closet feels like a private room in a Venetian palazzo, with its roman shades. Her son's room, on a different level, is very English – and Sasha's favourite room. 'I love the climbing vines,' she explains, 'and the green tones are soothing yet invigorating.' Her bedroom, papered in a Pierre Frey leopard design, is very Baroque in a cinematic way.

Throughout the house, European allusions are filtered through the energetic prism of New York City. This is a creative's townhouse with an Old World charm that connects to the neighbourhood and its architecture, but done in a fresh way. The inspiration behind the house may be English, French, Italian and more, but it could exist only in Manhattan. 'I was looking for inspiration at homes in Notting Hill, in Milan, and in the French countryside,' Sasha remembers. 'Mine is different from my sources, because I'm self-taught. It feels very free, without rules and boundaries. Although my work pays homage to the past, it's still a young approach.' She aims to design unique spaces, and believes that is what inspires her to create new visions and interiors. 'When I'm decorating for myself,' she explains, 'I don't overthink the process. I go with my instinct.' But she also believes that design is 'never done. I'm constantly changing and creating new spaces for myself. Design is not something that you stick with forever, and as our tastes evolve, we experiment and try new things. Things are always shifting, because it's my joy. Yet design is like a buffer where you want to try everything, and you don't do it.' In this case, it seems Sasha has done her house just right.

'French space-age furniture, 1980s Memphis Milano, Art Deco, 1970s Italian – I love it all. The mixing trick is always to let your passion and heart drive what you are buying. If you love it, buy it, and you'll find a way to make it work.'

JUXTAPOSITION / *I like to say the process of creating juxtapositions is like a game of connect the dots. When it comes to objects, I weave together pieces through the use of colour, material, pattern and texture; form, design or period are less important. The living room started with the colours of the Le Manach wallpaper, and all the elements are linked via colour.*

BALANCE / *Balance is created through colour and texture. Your eye shouldn't stop on one spot; it should be able to move seamlessly through the room. One piece should draw you to the next.*

SURPRISE / *The element of surprise comes from personal touches that are usually statement pieces and stand out among the more basic palate-cleansers. These flourishes are driven by shape and form. To me, a statement piece is one thing that is unexpected in the room. The coffee table in my living room, for instance, is a highly contemporary piece in a spectrum of colours. It works because it creates a pleasing jolt against the more traditional wallpaper.*

COLOUR / *Colour is important because it breathes life into a room. It is chosen in many ways. In my case it can start with a Persian rug as in the living room, or interesting historic wallpaper.*

PATTERN / *The colours of each pattern should complement and balance each other.*

TEXTURE / *Layering textures is a harmonising process. You want to provide a little bit of everything and not have one texture overpower the others.*

MOOD / *The mood is joyful – this is a happy house.*

LIMITATIONS & POSSIBILITIES / *When I bought and moved into the townhouse it had already been completely renovated. I didn't redo the floors or kitchen because they had recently been modernised and I was pregnant, so I made use of what I had and painted the kitchen cabinetry. Yes, it was challenging because I was pregnant, but I was able to get to the fun part and start decorating. Whatever I had to do, I had to make the existing elements disappear. I lacquered the kitchen cabinets blue, which transformed the room. Between the wallpaper and the paint, the marble that I would not have selected was made more interesting. The flooring on the raised ground floor was a commercial terrazzo. I covered it with carpet, and job done.*

ALL THINGS CONSIDERED / *I love that it has charm.*

SOPHIE DRIES
4ième, Paris

The French architect and designer Sophie Dries is known for her architectural projects, ceramic work and exceptional limited-edition furniture pieces commissioned by international galleries. Her interiors, which are dreamed up with a great respect for history and context, are guided by a deep sense of place. This immersive approach allows her to understand and shape balanced, coherent yet daring rooms.

Home is a spacious apartment in a 19th-century building in Paris's Marais district, where she lives with her husband, Marc Leschelier, who is an artist, and their young daughter. The building is set on a wide tree-lined boulevard; there are influential design concept stores just around the corner, and a mix of art galleries, foodie destinations and interesting fashion. 'I like to go out, but also enjoy the quieter aspect of the area and gravitate towards places that have a very low profile,' says Sophie. 'I like that the neighbourhood has culture and is not too bourgeois yet.'

The building's oxblood-coloured doors, some with time-worn masks, suggest a certain solid respectability, which is true to a point when one enters Sophie's stimulating apartment. The inspiration for the interiors is decidedly classical, and looking around at the contemporary and 1980s/90s pieces, one sees symmetry and a respect for the traditional codes of furniture placement. The rooms are supported by a formal layout, yet this is achieved only with contemporary art and design. 'There is symmetry and good proportion, even in the Stampa mirror above the mantel, which was designed to the right proportion,' explains Sophie. 'I've transposed classic codes but followed them with contemporary treatments. For example, consoles made from blocks of cement sit on the sophisticated marquetry of the wooden floors. I like it when raw meets refined. I enjoy the contrast and seeing what happens. This encounter creates a different emotion in every person.'

Sophie is drawn to textures and materials, and experiments with plaster, metal and wood. Her interior is about materiality, and her designs in collaboration with trusted workshops in France and Italy are made to sit in very specific spaces across the light-painted apartment. In particular, she loves the green room, a small space that previously had no function. She feels that it has a special atmosphere: 'I've created a room [in which] to read and be introspective. The lamp in metal is by my husband. The wall is covered in Japanese straw, backed by paper that is dyed a dark green. Small rooms that are dark become intimate. The green has an old castle vibe. Green makes you calmer.' She has left the original floor and fireplace untouched. 'Here and across the apartment I like to see the historic plaster mouldings, parquet, marble and fireplaces,' she explains.

Sophie sees her interior as an experiment. 'In the dining room there is a table where the table should be, for example, but the sorts of pieces are unexpected,' she says. 'I want to experiment with elements and go beyond boundaries in my home. The best way to push classic design is to live the way I live today, and this is how I live in a historic building. I like to mix eras and materials that are considered noble with materials that are not.' It is through this twist of contemporary and radical shapes and furniture in the context of a Haussmann interior that Sophie keeps things exciting.

'I like to respect symmetry and proportion, to have a precise architectural plan, then I shake things up by breaking the symmetry and mixing eras and materials, and by not being so serious.'

'My interior is a self-portrait painted with classical brushstrokes and very contemporary colours. Find your own path – there's no need to copy everything that already exists.'

JUXTAPOSITION / *Most of the objects in here, I have designed for the apartment or had tailor-made for each room. I feel it when it is right, as with the 'Meteor' rug that I created to travel around the bed. The mix happens first in my head.*

BALANCE / *I keep things disciplined and have objects in storage. Every house is unique, and although things can have a new story, not every object can move to another spot. I have pieces that were created to fit a specific space and that were made for this interior. Some pieces – art, and objects that are more sculptural – can travel to new homes.*

SURPRISE / *Art brings an element of surprise, when one is not too much of a fetishist about perfect taste. Known art often does not look fresh. Personality and surprise come through going beyond established good taste.*

COLOUR / *I'm not particularly into colour, but my interiors are not white. I'm more into dark colours: aubergine, dark grey, dark orange. I'm not Pop.*

PATTERN / *I like patterns that come from nature, such as marble or wood, or a patina on metal or mirror.*

TEXTURE / *I'm obsessed with texture. I always want to torture a material with fire or heat, for example, and try different processes. As a child I wanted to be a chemist, and I express that interest through my designs.*

MOOD / *There is great sensuality. I like the contrast between warm surfaces and those that are cold. In our apartment you want to touch the materials, even those objects that look sharp and almost dangerous.*

LIMITATIONS & POSSIBILITIES / *The structure of the apartment was there, and the original features, such as the parquet, the mouldings and the layout. These were things that we had to adhere to. I've not been afraid to experiment or to use unconventional materials that you would not expect in this building, to add contrast and surprises.*

ALL THINGS CONSIDERED / *I love the light that filters through the apartment, and the fact that the vibe changes from one room to another because of their different sizes and functions.*

ALEXANDRA TOLSTOY

Cotswolds, Oxfordshire

Anglo-Russian adventurer, author and television presenter Alexandra Tolstoy organises riding holidays in Kyrgyzstan and runs The Tolstoy Edit, a curated shop of her favourite interior discoveries. Her home, which dates from 1720, is nestled in a tiny hamlet of former farmworkers' cottages, down an idyllic winding road deep in the English countryside. 'I love it for its simplicity and remoteness,' she says, 'much more real than the nearby Cotswolds, and that we step straight out into fields. Its voice is unpretentious and rural. I selected it for this. It's a haven from the modern world for me, my children and our dog.'

A path through the pretty garden leads into the house via a small porch, past boots left casually by the door, and into the inviting kitchen with its worn flagstone floors and Aga. This romantic building, however, is no rustic cottage. Close observation reveals well-placed lamps and practical bright lights on kitchen counters, beautifully upholstered furniture and a mix of fabrics and ambience that would make set designers and the editors of glossy magazines swoon. Alexandra's home is a well-conceived, personal English country house on a small scale, where everything is of good quality, made and chosen with integrity, and well finished.

The interior style is sympathetic to the building. Alexandra's cottage is very different from her rented house in London, a Victorian townhouse where she has played much more with her Central Asian travels and Russian heritage. 'I like to be respectful to the roots of a house,' she explains, 'and the cottage has an English Laurie Lee feel,' she says, referencing the work of the poet and novelist.

Alexandra believes the adorable interiors of Alison Uttley's charming *Little Grey Rabbit* books, which she enjoyed as a child and now reads to her own children, seeped into her consciousness from very early on: 'Staffordshire dogs, patchwork quilts, gingham tablecloths – I hadn't realised until recently what an influence *Little Grey Rabbit* has been!'

The living room has a faint air of woodsmoke, as though the fire has recently been put out, and the windows are open to let in the scent of the countryside. The collections of ceramics and other objects – perhaps the result of Alexandra's habit of living life to the fullest and surrounding herself with the things for which she has a passion – look as though they would have taken many lifetimes to assemble.

Directing us up the stairs, Alexandra says, 'I have wallpaper in my bedroom, and the furniture there is a bit grander, as it's a bigger room.' The woodwork throughout the cottage is a glossy dark brown, she says explaining the colour palette: 'In my outside office, I continued the glossy brown to join it in spirit to the cottage, but otherwise completely broke the pattern with egg-yolk-yellow walls, pictures and coloured pieces from my travels along the Silk Road.'

There is a feeling of comfort and informality throughout the cottage. 'This is a home for my children,' Alexandra explains, 'and one that has stayed an unchanging constant during their lives. I absolutely love every room and every corner. I have owned it for twenty years now and little has changed in that time, so each object is a familiar friend. I think it's cosy. A Russian priest once visited us and said it feels like a mushroom that sprang from the ground – there is a feeling of timelessness, I hope. The ideas of "design" and a cottage don't work together. A cottage was built as a simple home and feels much more authentic sticking to this precept.'

'Being true to yourself is one of the most important elements of an interior. For me, fashion and interiors are oxymoronic. An interior reflects your personality, life and interests.'

'Antiques are important.
I've collected along the way
– many from local antiques
shops, some inherited, and
some from [Kensington
antiques shop] The Lacquer
Chest. They aren't serious
antiques, but decorative –
suited to the simple origins
of the cottage.'

JUXTAPOSITION / *I don't try in this way. I collect things that I love: a group of lustre jugs, endless Staffordshire dogs, 19th-century embroidered pictures, sailors' Valentines …*

BALANCE / *It's impossible to be totally tidy with three children! But I do like having people round for supper, because it makes me tidy up. In this respect, lots of antiques are much more forgiving than a minimalist interior.*

SURPRISE / *Many people nowadays seem to go for a rather generic 'country' look, with well-known paint colours and lots of tongue-and-groove, so my brown furniture and lustreware are quite surprising. But my decorating isn't to create an effect, but rather to showcase the things I love.*

COLOUR / *I stayed true to the roots of the cottage and replaced the modern plaster with lime plaster, with a simple white limewash everywhere. As would have happened traditionally, I rewash it when it gets too dirty. This wasn't just for looks, but also for practicality – the cottage is much less damp as a result.*

PATTERN / *Generally, I like to have a common colour running through the mixed patterns. In my office, it's a rich red that I have adored all my life.*

TEXTURE / *I love the contrast of the chalkiness of the lime plaster and the oak furniture – there is definitely no polishing of furniture! The curtains are cotton, and all the textures feel earthy and natural.*

MOOD / *It takes you back in time or out of time to a simpler life. I spent my twenties riding horses for months on end through Central Asia, Mongolia and Siberia, and fell in love with the simplicity of living for the day. It's difficult to find this feeling in everyday life, but at my cottage I do find it. I don't drive, so my children and I just cook, walk, head to the River Thames, play cards, read books … it's a slice of heaven.*

LIMITATIONS & POSSIBILITIES / *It's a small space for four of us, but I've used every single possibility. I'm about to make the outside office into a bedroom for my oldest son, as the children have been sharing a room until now. Last year I asked [cabin-maker] Rollo Dunford Wood to build a wonderful corrugated-iron shed in the garden. It's given us another room, and it looks as though it's always been there.*

ALL THINGS CONSIDERED / *My cottage hasn't changed. It has been the most constant and familiar friend to me and my children.*

NATALIA MIYAR /

/ *Coral Gables, Florida*

Shaded by the lush, cocooning branches of tall oaks, stopper and ashoka trees, the home of London architect and designer Natalia Miyar is an architectural landmark in the historic 'Italian Village' of Coral Gables, Florida, a garden city adjacent to bustling Miami. Natalia's home away from her UK base sits discreetly in a charming neighbourhood of verdant lawns, wide streets and Mediterranean Revival character, an oasis in the heart and heat of southern Florida.

'I love that my house is a garden house,' says Natalia, who was born in Mexico to Cuban parents, sitting in the living room overlooking the tropical foliage. 'The garden affects the whole feel of my home. I love to spend time in it, and it is so peaceful and private. Even when I am not in the garden, I am in a room overlooking it.' The L-shape of the building means that all rooms lead out on to a beautiful side yard, and most have windows on three walls. 'I am surrounded by beautiful Florida vegetation from Jamaica capers to silver buttonwoods. It really feels as though I am living in a garden – my own peaceful retreat.'

This is Natalia's principal residence when she is in Miami for work, and is also an escape that she often shares with family and friends. Known as 'Palmarito', the house lends itself to entertaining and hosting – which, along with spending time in the garden, is one of her passions. Dating from 1925, it was designed by Robert Law Weed, a Miami architect otherwise known for his modernist projects. 'I fell in love with the layout and character of the building,' Natalia recalls. 'It had incredible bones and so much potential. The rooms were beautifully proportioned, most have windows on three walls, so you feel the vibrancy of the nature outside within the house. The layout is very clever, maximising cool breezes. I stripped back all the years of inauthenticity to reveal the original historic character and integrity of the building, and added my own touches.'

The inspiration was the Florida landscape, a palette of greens and blues that embodies Natalia's love of nature. The secondary inspiration was her art collection, which tells the story of her interests and travels. The collection is culturally varied, full of texture and colour. Most of the objects were collected over time, and Natalia purchased very little specifically for this house. Not surprisingly, her collection grows and evolves as she explores new places.

Natalia's style is a blend of comfort and glamour, creating interiors that are easy to live in but with a vibrancy introduced through strong art, accessories and a reflection of her personality. The focus is on natural textures and materials, which feel very serene against the backdrop of the outside space. A rich colour palette brings balance, warmth and character that make people feel comfortable and at home in the house. Natalia adores having guests, and they cannot wait to just breathe out and relax. Clearly this is a space people don't want to leave.

'I am definitely a collector. My favourite way to accessorise a room is with a collection of pieces that have meaning and history... My favourite objects are my art collection. I am endlessly inspired by art, and I have chosen these pieces over many years. They are a reflection of my character. I enjoy living with the things that I love and what I am intuitively connected to.'

'Designing my own home was an opportunity to enjoy the design process, creating a setting for my extensive collection.'

'Everything has been
chosen and designed by
me, so it is entirely personal.
It is an accumulation of my
experiences and creative
outlook. The furniture is
bespoke and designed by
me as well.'

JUXTAPOSITION / *The goal was to create harmonious contrast. You achieve that by finding a common thread, perhaps a material or texture. I love to work with materials that are unexpected but perhaps all have an interesting or similar texture.*

BALANCE / *I don't enjoy living in a messy space, so I always try to keep my house quite put-together. I enjoy sitting in a room and looking at a composition, playing around with it, adding something new – or removing something, which can be as impactful as adding.*

SURPRISE / *Make sure the items in your home resonate with you. This always feels authentic and stops the place from looking contrived or stiff. I don't like mass-produced objects; I like my home to tell a story. They don't have to be expensive, but I want to see beautifully crafted objects.*

COLOUR / *Colour is hugely important to me; it informs so much in my practice. I always want my home to be filled with the colour I love. The palette here reflects the vibrant Florida landscape and, of course, the surrounding gardens that are such an important part of my home.*

PATTERN / *I rarely use a material without a pattern (unless it's velvet) as I think it adds interest to every piece. Playing with scale is important when mixing patterns. My dining room has an oversized printed and hand-foiled pattern on the walls in the form of my 'Ambia' wallcovering, created with British brand Fromental's artists in the UK. I used a moire material on the chairs for visual interest and contrast without competing with the walls.*

TEXTURE / *I love to layer textures and finishes – it adds great depth and interest. Here, I used natural materials, all of which have their own special qualities, such as deeply textured ebonised oak, leathered soapstone, amazonite, woven bamboo shades, layering them with fabrics and texture-enhancing light to create a subtle, unique space.*

MOOD / *The mood of my home is creative, calming and comfortable. It is a place I love to be in. I achieved this using colour, texture and lighting, which have created a tranquil and inviting space.*

LIMITATIONS & POSSIBILITIES / *All spaces have their restrictions and limitations, and that is often when we are at our most creative. My living room is particularly awkward, with an off-centre main window and a fireplace in the corner, so there is no natural centre. My 1970s travertine screen has transformed the room, and with clever styling and the thoughtful positioning of art, it is now one of my favourite spaces in the house. Idiosyncrasies are what add personality to a home, so they should be embraced.*

ALL THINGS CONSIDERED / *I travel frequently and spend a lot of time creating beautiful spaces for others to live in. To have a space to return to that feels authentic to me, where every object is something I love or has a personal story attached, is what I enjoy most. It is a place where my friends and family love to be, and is truly my sanctuary.*

JENNIFER SHORTO

Kensington, London

Cornwall Gardens in Kensington, London, is a pleasant, long square of elegant white Grade II listed buildings dating from 1870, shaded by some of the city's tallest plane trees. The neighbourhood feels peaceful, with the famous well-wooded gardens at its heart and neat rows of equally tall houses, many of which have been divided into apartments. The vibe is slightly formal yet creative, an area where one often hears the sound of people practising musical instruments, and where classic cars are parked on the street.

We ascend the stairs of one of these stucco-fronted houses to meet the textile and wallpaper designer Jennifer Shorto, founder of her eponymous company. French-American by birth, Jennifer has spent time in Brazil, Mexico, Paris, Brussels and London, and her professional work reflects this, as well as drawing from her extensive collection of antique textiles. Her designs blend historical and contemporary influences, and in her home with the living space at the top and the bedrooms on the lower floor, we are seemingly visually transported to Paris via a relaxed, sunny Brazilian sensibility. 'I live here with my second husband, but the property was originally decorated for me and my children before we were married,' she says of the light-filled two-storey apartment. 'We moved in as [the children] were finishing school and entering university. It's a very feminine and playful space.'

Jennifer describes the style of her home as 'luxurious bohemian'. One could add 'well-travelled art collector', with thrilling contemporary art balanced by layers of fascinating textiles. Here, well-proportioned traditional antiques meet controlled flourishes, such as the green Memphis Group table by Ettore Sottass. 'Part of the inspiration behind the interior was to test my new wallpapers in various small rooms,' explains Jennifer, 'ensuring a harmonious flow from one room to the next, especially with the open-plan living room on the top floor flooded with natural light.' In the living room, her 'Emeralds' wallpaper with its graphically placed insects waiting to be discovered provides an amusing yet stylish backdrop.

'I love my bedroom, because it's a golden box that shimmers with the sun streaming through the tall trees,' she says as we survey the 'Golden Bees' wallpaper, which evokes old Spanish embossed leather, yet feels very current. 'People are often surprised when they visit, because they climb up a crazy number of floors and suddenly find themselves in what seems like a completely different house with light streaming in from above. It resembles an artist's studio floating above a forest with a garden on the roof.'

'The spirit I wanted to create in my family home was relaxed and fun. Mixing periods and styles encourages that feeling, and so do drawings. They bring to mind the artist's studio, where ideas are first explored and developed in a series of sketches before taking shape in the final oil painting. My home feels like a studio, and having drawings around reinforces that creative atmosphere.'

'My home is very bohemian chic. There are rugs everywhere, ceramics, sculptures, drawings, and of course antique fabrics.'

JUXTAPOSITION / *I approach interiors like gardens, focusing on creating points of view that interact harmoniously. For example, my bedroom is a small, intimate space filled with objects and drawings that invite close inspection. It evolved naturally to feature many portraits, depictions of hands, and even the golden mask of a Chinese princess, creating interesting and cohesive vignettes.*

BALANCE / *I live in a small space, so I edit constantly. Especially my clothes!*

SURPRISE / *They are personal objects I've gathered through my life. I can't say how they differ, but I seem to sway between very old, such as Tang dynasty ceramics, and fairly new, such as 20th-century modernist ceramics and sculpture.*

COLOUR / *Colour is always important, and in my home it is guided by the central 'Emeralds' wallpaper that dominates throughout. It has mainly green and touches of blue. A lot of the furniture consequently ended up being cobalt and Prussian blues and emerald-greens. Dispersed touches of red give the space rhythm.*

PATTERN / *Colour was more important than pattern. I just made sure that they were quite open patterns, so everything could breathe.*

TEXTURE / *I'm very attached to the presence of West African textiles, and art is always very present in my life. West African textiles are a love of mine that endures through time. I find their relaxed sophistication and their use of colour masterful. As for art, it's always been part of who I am. Whether I'm painting myself, collecting pieces or selling others' work, art is woven into the fabric of my life.*

MOOD / *The mood is joyful and warm, and a large part of this feeling is because of the exuberance of the colours. The blue is very much a cobalt-blue, the green is emerald, the red vermilion.*

LIMITATIONS & POSSIBILITIES / *I believe wallpaper can open spaces that are confined, which is often the case in London. The challenge with my home was that the main staircase led directly into the living room, meaning the wallpaper needed to flow seamlessly between the two areas without being overwhelming. Thankfully, it turned out light-hearted and easy, creating a unified and inviting atmosphere.*

ALL THINGS CONSIDERED / *My home is wonderfully peaceful and, being level with the top of the trees, I get a lot of light and a lot of nature. I see the little green parakeets in the trees in front of my bedroom, which is heaven. It is a home that was made for my children, warm and unprecious, filled with love.*

FRANCIS SULTANA /

Mayfair, London

'My apartment is right in the heart of central London – my local shop is renowned retailer Fortnum & Mason – but while I am close to everything, my home is also an oasis, hidden away,' says the Maltese-British interior designer and gallerist Francis Sultana. His building, the Albany, just off Piccadilly, was built in the 18th century by the architect Sir William Chambers. A highly desirable building, it has traditionally been a home for bachelors, and even today the residents are not allowed to have children under 12 or pets, lending it an air that is simultaneously grand, solid, rakish and artistic. Politicians, philanthropists, artists, designers and many others – from British prime minister William Gladstone to Lord Byron – have called this unique building home. 'It's a perfect pied-à-terre, like living in a hotel without living in a hotel, historic and practical, at the centre of London,' Francis explains. This particular set (as the apartments in the Albany are called) was previously owned by the American writer and editor Fleur Cowles, who was known for her influential magazine *Flair* in the 1950s. Francis shares the apartment with his partner of many years, the visionary gallerist David Gill, founder of David Gill Gallery, one of the world's foremost dealers of leading contemporary art and design.

Sitting on a comfortable sofa in the Blue Salon, Francis describes himself as a curator: 'As an interior designer I create homes that reflect my clients, their passions and the needs of them and their families. Craftsmanship, authenticity and longevity are my keywords. I don't follow trends slavishly, but seek to create spaces that will stand the test of time.' His set is one of London's most exciting private spaces, with a mix of museum-worthy art and design that feels at home in the historic rooms. 'I need to push my boundaries all the time,' he says. 'Although I don't experiment on clients, I do experiment on myself, whether from a contemporary or a historical narrative. I have always looked back, even while working with contemporary designers. In the Albany I wanted to create something that is relevant today while respecting the past.'

Following much research, Francis restored the set and combined two large apartments, with great respect. The Blue Salon is his favourite room, where he socialises, and also where he works from home. 'This is a historical room, yet I have crafted a room for today, using the colour of the 18th century. I wanted to create something here on a par from the aesthetics point of view, something that captures a moment in design.'

While the Blue Salon is a great room for entertaining, with a formal vibe, the White Salon opposite feels more like a studio. 'This room had so few original features left,' says Francis, 'and it responds to David's need for a slightly off-white box for contemporary art. It is a space where we can enjoy the art collection in a more moveable way. We keep on changing things. It piles up and evolves.' The scheme for the dining room also required painstaking research and much refurbishment, but it fell into place when the original teal-blue was discovered, and now he is very happy with the result.

Upstairs, Francis inhabits the set's most serene space. 'My bedroom is cosier,' he explains. 'I need tranquillity, I have very little art and the works are small in scale. All furniture is by me, and this is my place of rest. My dressing room with a tub has the Neo-Romantic art we collected in the 1990s.'

In Francis' home, the eye doesn't stand still. The set has a controlled respect for the past, a desire to use traditional skills and craft, a love of merging the traditional with contemporary art and design, and an elegant use of colour and texture. 'Although individuality is an important element,' says Francis, 'I would hope that people visiting my home will remember the space with happiness and contentment, and feel a sensation of comfort and being cocooned.'

'I don't have rules, as I would always be breaking them! I can't be rigid; giving yourself parameters is limiting, and it's important to experiment and not have boundaries. Also, don't be afraid of moving with your look. Whether in my own work or when I commission pieces from an artist, I create something new through experimentation.'

'Looking at Art Deco in the early 20th century you discover its amazing quality. That quality helped its design and supported the people who created [these pieces].'

'Provocative pieces add to a scheme. I have no problem with something sexy and challenging. Disturbing the balance makes the balance.'

JUXTAPOSITION / *Colour is usually the link between objects, be that tonal or otherwise. Sometimes texture, sometimes a stylistic thread. It really depends on the pieces and the context.*

BALANCE / *Knowing when to stop is key! There is a fine line between curating pieces and objects to create balance, and adding too much so that the eye doesn't know where to land.*

SURPRISE / *I curate from my heart, so the mix changes depending on my mood. Equally, that's something we have always done at the gallery: mixing materials and eras to create something new and exciting.*

COLOUR / *I knew I wanted to use blue in the salon because I had researched the original colour palette of the period. I also wanted a white salon to show the Zaha Hadid liquid glacial pieces and the work by the Paris-based artist and designer Mattia Bonetti. The dining room has evolved, but now we have teal-blue walls and the artwork by Flora Yukhnovich, I am very happy with it.*

PATTERN / *I tend to use plains in the curtains, and let pattern appear in the art and other pieces, such as the rugs by Mattia Bonetti.*

TEXTURE / *Once the first phase of a room is done – walls and ceilings and carpets – I can start layering with texture and pattern. This has to work with the art and lighting as well, so each approach is very different. I have used tweed in my upholstery, bronze in my furniture and materials like mohair or kidassia goat fur. I love texture, and use it a lot in my upholstery. It adds the ultimate luxury to an interior, although the approach has to be measured.*

MOOD / *I want an interior to be elegant, to look considered yet not overly so, to work with the architecture and light on offer, but also – most importantly – to reflect and augment our lives so that we can enjoy the space, so that it works for us and the different moods we have from day to night.*

LIMITATIONS & POSSIBILITIES / *You must acknowledge them, but don't let them take over a design and your approach. If a space has limited light, for example, work with it, not against it.*

ALL THINGS CONSIDERED / *I've followed my approach to creating a home, from the consideration of the space itself to how you approach the decoration and the pieces you put in that space. Not following trends is key, looking to the past and to the future, and choosing great craftsmanship. I believe in making things to last. It is a great luxury, but well-made things also have a great life and carry on. In my own interior, I live with the pieces I have collected over the years, the furniture I have designed and the pieces I have commissioned. [It is these] that make the set personal. This apartment is a reflection of my journey.*

J.J. MARTIN Page 40: Set of 2 custom-made armchairs covered in Prada vintage green fabric by Holliday & Brown, 2000s, Italy; Left painting: *Goddess*, Ruben Toledo, 2000s; Right painting: *BAC*, 1960s; Vintage pair of bedside lamps, 1970s Murano glass (Cavalli & Nastri, Milan). **Page 42**: Vintage pavone chair painted cornflower blue (Penelope, Milan). **Page 43**: Set of 2 custom-made armchairs covered in Prada vintage green fabric by Holliday & Brown, 2000s, Italy; Red vase, Pierre Cardin, 1970s, Italy; *Goddess*, Ruben Toledo, 2000s; Right painting: *BAC*, 1960s; Upper left photo: Dimore Studio, 2000s; Upper left collage: Urn collage, Claire Johnson, 2019, Milan; Upper middle painting: Sorel's painting, 1950s; Upper right corner: Gagosian Art Gallery invitation; Lower right corner: Deer artwork, MM Paris; Vintage ottoman covered in David Hicks fabric; Custom-made footrest covered by Prada's reissued vintage fabric by Holliday & Brown; Chair, Carlo Ratti. **Pages 44–45**: Vintage table lamp, Franco Albini, 1960s, Italy (Cavalli & Nastri); Vintage red velvet couch, 1950s, Italy; Set of 2 wooden chairs, Carlo Ratti, 1950s, Italy (Spazio 900, Milan); Cousy couch, Artflex, covered in peacock blue velvet, 2000s, Italy; Vintage glass coffee tables (Navigli flea market, Milan); Antique yellow wool carpet, early 1900s, China, Rose Carpets, Milan; Dusty Rose paint colour custom-mixed by J.J.'s painter in Milan; Vintage Unicorn needlepoint artwork, 1970s, Italy (etsy.it); Vintage leather chairs, 1970s, Italy (Zucca Gallery, Pesaro, Italy); Vintage ottoman covered in David Hicks fabric; Left wall top two paintings, watercolours, Paolo Ferraguti; Left wall bottom two paintings, Italian, 1950s (Zucca Gallery, Milan); Pineapple bubble vase, La DoubleJ. **Page 46**: Plates and glasses, Rainbow series, La DoubleJ; Napkins, Wildbird Viola, La DoubleJ. **Page 47**: White tables, Molteni, Italy; Vintage bamboo chairs (subito.it); Chair cushions covered with 1920s Domino print fabric, La DoubleJ; 'Tree of Life' wallpaper, custom-made, from an illustration by Kirsten Synge; Herringbone intarsia original wood flooring, 1910; Murano glass ceiling lamp, 1950s, Italy (Moioli Gallery). **Pages 48–49**: Vintage bamboo table, early 1900s, Italy; Deruta vases and charger plate, custom-made; 'Tree of Life wallpaper, custom-made, from an illustration by Kirsten Synge. **Page 50**: Mirror, 8th century, Italy (church sale, Milan); Vintage Danish wood and glass cabinet, 19th century, (Six Gallery, Milan); Cabinet top shelf, glasses, Rainbow series, La DoubleJ; Chairs, Thonet, reupholstered with 1920s Domino print, La DoubleJ; Porcelain plates, prototypes, La DoubleJ; Carrara marble-top table, custom-made, 2000s, Italy; Pineapple bubble vase, La DoubleJ. **Page 51**: Vintage Danish wood and glass cabinet, 19th century, sourced from my friend Fanny at Six Gallery in Milan (filled on top shelf with La DoubleJ's rainbow Murano glass collection with Salviati); Vintage Thonet dining room chairs reupholstered with La DoubleJ's 1920s Domino print; a selection of prototypes of porcelain plates produced for La DoubleJ. **Pages 52–53**: Bamboo beds, 1970s, Italy (subito.it); Bed cushions, Transylvania private collection, Mickey Bombarta, and Botanical fabric, La DoubleJ; Bed linens, Ghidoli, Milan; Green paint custom-mixed by J.J.'s painter in Milan; Custom pillow cover, Botanical Print, La DoubleJ; Set of 2 brass table lamps, Rossi Oldrati, 1970s, Italy; From right to left: Oil paintings, Katrina Van Ike, 1940s, USA (J.J.'s great-grandmother); Embroidererd Spanish crown, 19th century; Illustration, Ruben Toledo; Pineapple bubble vase, La DoubleJ. **Page 54**: Neo Gothic wooden double mirror, 1970s, France. **Page 56**: Set of 2 pouffes covered in Slinky Rosso fabric, La DoubleJ, 2000s, Italy.

GERT VOORJANS Pages 70–71: Naturalistic chandelier and bronze botanical side tables, Clotilde Ancarani.

SOPHIE DRIES Page 191: Travertine stone dyed in blue, Sophie Dries; Artwork, Laurent Grasso & Deborah Bo. **Page 193**: *Styx* mirror metal, Sophie Dries; *Jingle* saw chair, Max Lamb; Painting, Ana Karkae; Large photo, Ryan McGinley; *Marble* console, Sophie Dries; Vase, Gaetano Pesce; Gasa suspension, Konstantin Grcic; Concrete artworks, Marc Leschelier; *Akari* lamp, Noguchi x Tom Sachs; Metal vase, Josef Hoffmann; Hemp sheers, SD edition. **Pages 194–195**: *Croissant* sofa, Sophie Dries; *Stampa* mirror, Sophie Dries; Concrete stool, Marc Leschelier; Artwork, Thomas Lélu; Black wood chair, Paolo Palluco. **Pages 196–197**: Vintage desk, BPPR (Nilufar Gallery); Metal lamp, Marc Leschelier; Chair, Alvar Aalto; *Night* stand and *Meteor* rug, Sophie Dries; Wood *Pop* chair, Serban Ionescu. **Page 198**: Chandelier *Glow*, Sophie Dries for Kaia Lighting; Table, *Songye*, Sophie Dries; Chairs, Philippe Starck, 1986; *Traces* vases and Candle holder, Sophie Dries. **Page 199**: Coffee table, Max Lamb; Concrete stool, Marc Leschelier; *Stampa* mirror and Croissant sofa, Sophie Dries. **Pages 200–201**: Metal lamp, Marc Leschelier. **Page 202**: Chair, Gaetano Pesce; *Traces* Rug, Sophie Dries (Nilufar Gallery).

NATALIA MIYAR Pages 224–225: Painting, *Untitled*, Adler Guerrier; Dibujo Tejido 11 textile, Daniela Libertad; Earthenware terracotta items *Le Temps est à L'Orage* & *L'Ange Gabriel*, Aude Van Ryn (The New Craftsmen); Tray by Reinaldo Sanguino. **Page 226**: *L'Arbe Grave* & *L'Arbe Grave #3* blue engravings, Edouard Duval (Carrie). **Page 227**: Silkscreen painting, Moises Finale. **Page 230**: *Spouts and Holes* Vessel, Priscilla Hollingsworth; Sculpture in raw biscuit of porcelain and hemp, Benedicte Vallet. **Page 231**: Sculpture in Raw Biscuit of Porcelain and Hemp by Benedicte Vallet; Stool, Reinaldo Sanguino; *Personage* collage, Pepe Mar; *Untitled* acrylic, Magnus Sodamin. **Page 232**: Haiku painted timber, Dan Schneiger. **Pages 234–235**: *In My Mind, in My Head I Wanted it to Happen Sleepwalker, Where Do you Belong* acrylic by Vickie Peierre. **Page 236–237**: *Calle Cuba* photograph, Victoria Montoro.

JENNIFER SHORTO Pages 242–250: All wallpapers and fabrics, Jennifer Shorto or antique; Pages 242–243: Etchings, Lucian Freud; David Hockney; Pages 244–250: Leon Kossoff; Frank Auerbach; Raymond Pettibon; Jim Dine; Mario Schiffano.

FRANCIS SULTANA Pages 250–268: Shelves, Sebastian Errazuriz; Rug and mirror, Mattia Bonetti; Furniture and lighting, Francis Sultana and Mattia Bonetti; Artworks, Paul McCarthy, Chris Offili.

ACKNOWLEDGEMENTS

Emilio Pimentel-Reid

I would first like to thank the designers and creatives whose houses are shown in this book. The delight I receive from your work encourages me to collaborate with talented people and champion the design industry.

Equally *All Things Considered* would not have been possible without the beautiful images shot by Edvinas Bruzas. His thoughtful photography captures the personality, flair, joy and subtlety of these interiors.

The following individuals deserve great credit for the creation of *All Things Considered*: Kate Burkett at Quadrille who commissioned this book; I could not have asked for a better editor and thank her for her energy, stimulus and reassurance. Rosanna Fairhead for her sensitive editing and Roger Barnard whose graphic ingenuity helps tell our stories.

To all my clients as well as my colleagues with whom I've had the pleasure to work, past and present. Likewise, I owe so much to my mentors Mark Casertano, Joseph Holtzman and Vicente Wolf, without whose individual visions, creativity and sprinkling of magic and encouragement at different stages of my professional life I would not have discovered my world of interiors.

To my friends Jose Ramon Reyes and Mark Tennyson-d'Eyncourt, who put up with my extravagances and are always there for brainstorming ideas. And to JLD who accompanies me on this adventure.

Finally, I dedicate this book to my mother Georgiana Reid, whose love for art, interiors and beauty and her house filled with antiques, memories, books and design magazines in the Dominican Republic stays inside me always and inspires me to this day.

Emilio Pimentel-Reid is an Author, Creative Director and Brand Strategist.

As a design industry authority Emilio has over 25 years of experience collaborating with some of the world's most recognised high-end publications and interior style brands.

An advocate for British design and manufacturing, Emilio's Studio Pimentel-Reid advises leading architectural and design practices, interior brands, retailers and emerging talent in the areas of brand strategy, market positioning, style and product development.

As an award-winning Interiors Stylist and Creative Director he has delivered compelling content across print and digital platforms, trend-led events and hosted client experiences for high-end interior style brands, retailers, online platforms, international design fairs and large corporate organisations.

Emilio's insightful editorial features and styled shoots have appeared in the pages of British and international editions of ELLE Decoration, Architectural Digest, the Sunday Times Style, GQ and Harper's Bazaar, among others. He is an industry commentator, panellist, moderator and has judged graduate work at British design schools.

Quadrille, Penguin Random House UK,
One Embassy Gardens, 8 Viaduct Gardens, London SW11 7BW

Quadrille Publishing Limited is part of the Penguin Random House
group of companies whose addresses can be found at
global.penguinrandomhouse.com

Published by Quadrille in 2025

www.penguin.co.uk

A CIP catalogue record for this book is available from the British Library

ISBN 9781784887391
10 9 8 7 6 5 4 3 2 1

Publishing Director Kate Pollard
Senior Commissioning Editor Kate Burkett
Copy Editor Rosie Fairhead
Proof Reader Clare Double
Internal Design Roger Barnard | Velvet Design Associates
Cover Design Stuart Hardie
Photographers Edvinas Bruzas; Robyn Lea (pages 40, 43, 46, 48–49, 52–53, 55 and 56);
Barbara Franzò (pages 42, 44–45, 47, 50, 51 and 54); Nin Solis (pages 74–89); Manu Rodriguez (pages 176 and 183);
Chris Mottalini (pages 178–179, 180, 181, 182, 184, 185 and 186) and Simon Brown (pages 222–239)
Production Controller Martina Georgieva

Colour reproduction by p2d

Printed in China by C&C Offset Printing Co., Ltd.

The authorised representative in the EEA is Penguin Random House Ireland,
Morrison Chambers, 32 Nassau Street, Dublin D02 YH68.

Penguin Random House is committed to a sustainable future for our business, our readers and our planet.
This book is made from Forest Stewardship Council® certified paper.